Written and Illustrated by Caroline Arnold

A Day and Night in the AMAZON RAINFOREST

raintree
a Capstone company — publishers for children

6:00 A.M.

Cricka, cricka! call the toucans. Time to wake up!

It is early morning in the Amazon rainforest. The noisy birds hop from branch to branch, looking for food. They find ripe fruit and pick it with their long bills.

A toucan's call can be heard up to 0.8 kilometres away. Howler monkeys can be heard as far away as 4.8 kilometres.

The eerie calls of a troop of howler monkeys fill the air. These large monkeys are looking for food, too. They swing through the trees, holding on with their hands, feet and tails. They find fresh leaves and settle down to eat.

9:00 A.M.

An iguana sits in a patch of sunlight and warms its scaly body. Its spiny back warns other animals to stay away. Then, gripping branches with its long claws, the iguana searches for flowers, fruit and leaves to eat.

A snake's jaws can separate, allowing it to swallow food larger than the width of its body.

Near by, an emerald tree boa hangs from a branch. It hides among the green leaves. The snake waits for a bird or small animal to come close. Quick as a wink, it snatches its prey in its wide jaws and swallows it whole.

MIDDAY

Coatis scamper along the shady forest floor. They snort, scream and whistle to one another. They look for leaves, fruit and nuts up in the trees and on the ground. Coatis will eat almost anything, including insects and dead animals. But they stay away from the colourful poison frogs!

More than 1,000 types of frog live in the Amazon rainforest. They catch insects with their long tongues. The tiny poison frogs are active only during the day. Their skin is poisonous. The frogs' bright colours warn predators not to eat them.

Coatis are related to raccoons. They use their long tails for balance as they climb.

3:00 P.M.

The air feels thick and sticky. Clouds gather, and rain falls. High in the trees, a sleeping sloth hangs from a branch. When the rain stops, the sloth opens its eyes. It slowly reaches for a leaf. It slowly munches the leaf. Then it curls up and goes to sleep again.

Sloths do everything slowly. Their slow movements make it harder for predators to spot them. Sloths are the main food for harpy eagles. When an eagle finds a sloth, it grabs it with its powerful talons.

Harpy eagles are some of the largest birds in the world. Their talons are more than 13 centimetres long!

6:00 P.M.

Shadows grow long. Day-time animals look for safe places to spend the night. Night-time animals wake up.

A giant armadillo comes out of its burrow. It finds a termite mound and digs into it with its strong feet and claws. The termites scurry, but the armadillo catches them with its long, sticky tongue.

Near by, an ocelot yawns and stretches its legs. It listens for the sounds of small animals. All night long it will prowl the forest looking for prey.

The ocelot's eyes contain a layer called the tapetum. It reflects light and helps the ocelot to see in the dark.

9:00 P.M.

Bats find their way in the dark by listening to the echoes of their own sounds. This is called echolocation.

The moon rises over the tops of the trees. Bats flap their wings and take off into the cool night. Some swoop after insects. Others look for flowers and fruit. Vampire bats search for blood.

Owl monkeys climb through the high branches. Their large eyes help them to see in the dark. They search for flowers, fruit, insects and leaves. A moth flies by, and a monkey snatches it and eats it.

MIDNIGHT

On the damp forest floor, a tarantula comes out of its burrow. Tapirs grab twigs, shoots, fruits and berries with their long snouts. Deer nibble leaves among the bushes. As the deer and tapirs search for food, they watch and listen for hungry jaguars.

Tarantulas are the biggest spiders in the world. Some have bodies more than 8 centimetres long and legs up to 13 centimetres.

Jaguars slip through the shadows on silent paws. Their spots help them to hide. When a jaguar gets close to its prey, it pounces and bites it with powerful jaws.

3:00 A.M.

Night-time is busy along the banks of rainforest rivers and streams. An anaconda lurks at the water's edge. It waits for a deer, capybara or another animal to come for a drink. The huge snake will grab its prey, squeeze it to death, and swallow it whole.

Anacondas can grow to be about 9 metres long.

On the other side of the river, capybaras splash and look for water plants. They eat and rest all through the night. When morning comes they settle down to sleep for the day.

6:00 A.M.

The sky gets light, and night-time animals get ready to rest. Bats fold their wings, the ocelot and jaguar curl up for a nap, and the armadillo goes back into its burrow. Day-time animals open their eyes and start a new day.

Cricka, cricka! call the toucans. Monkeys chatter. Lizards and snakes climb on forest branches.

Every day and every night, animals find food, water and safe places to rest in the Amazon rainforest. It provides them with everything they need.

What is a tropical rainforest?

A tropical rainforest is a thick forest where rain falls nearly every day. The trees grow tall. The climate is warm all year.

The tall trees form a roof-like canopy that can be 30 metres above the ground. Some scattered trees can reach heights of 46 metres. The canopy is home to amphibians, reptiles, birds and mammals. Some live their entire lives in the canopy, without ever touching the ground.

Branches of the rainforest trees are covered with plants. Ferns, mosses, bromeliads and orchids grow there. Bromeliads have a large tank of water at the base of their leaves. Many insects, spiders, frogs and salamanders live in bromeliads.

The forest floor is covered with a thick layer of fallen leaves called leaf litter. Insects, rodents, frogs, snakes and other animals live on the forest floor.

Throughout the day and night, animals are busy in the rainforest. Diurnal animals are active during the day. Nocturnal animals are active at night. Which animals in this book are diurnal? Which are nocturnal? Where do they live in the rainforest?

Where can you find tropical rainforests?

Tropical rainforests are found in Central and South America, Africa, Asia and Australia. Most are near the equator. The Amazon rainforest in South America is the biggest rainforest in the world.

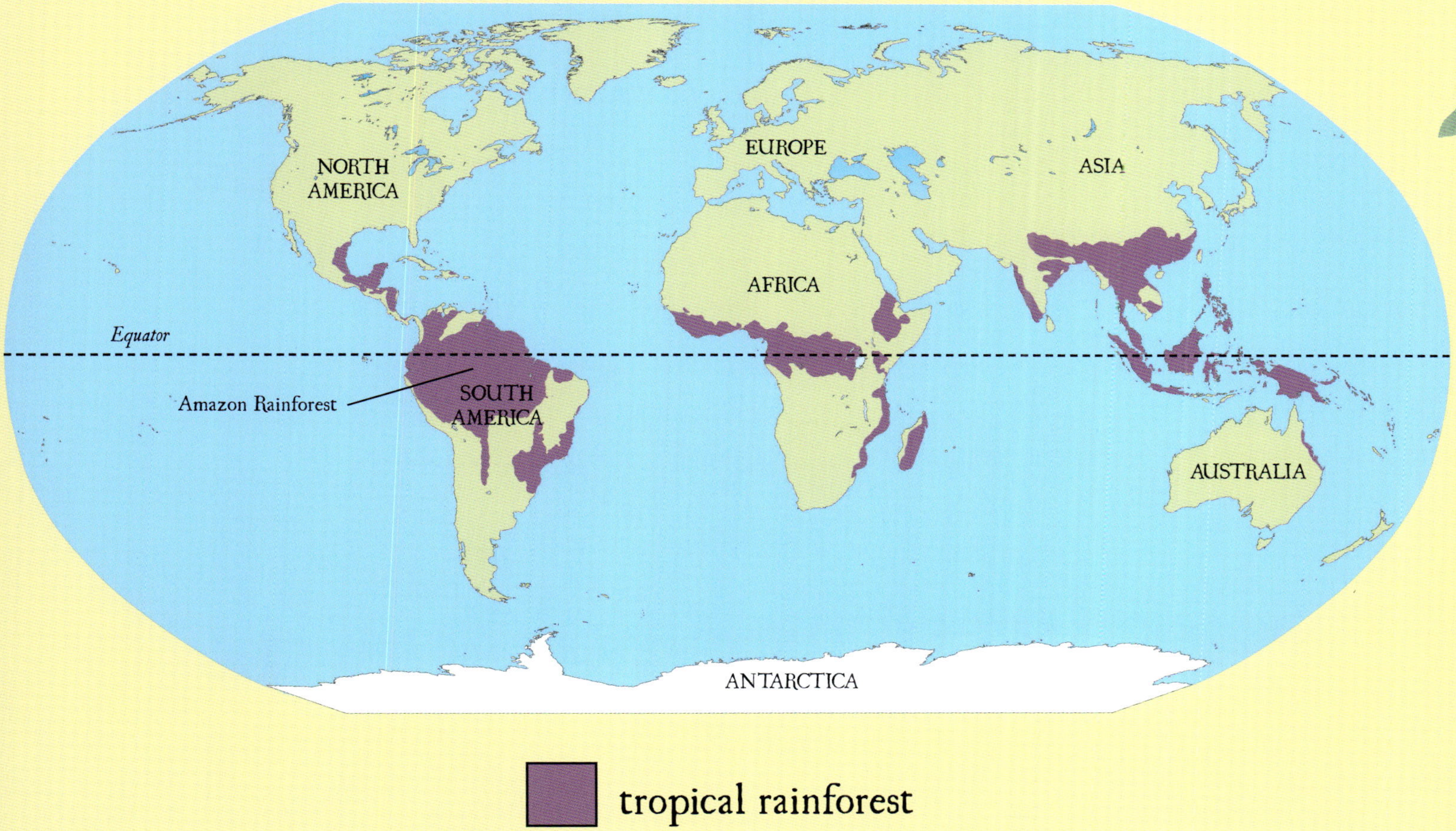

Fun Facts

- Iguanas can grow up to 2 metres long. They are among the largest lizards in the rainforest.
- Adult emerald tree boas are green, just as their name suggests. But the young snakes are orange. They change colour as they get bigger.
- Sloths have extra bones in their necks. The bones allow the sloths to swivel their heads almost completely around.
- "Armadillo" is a Spanish word that means "little armoured one". Bony plates cover the armadillo's body and protect it from predators.
- Owl monkeys are also called night monkeys. They are the only nocturnal monkeys in the Americas.
- Tapirs often live near rivers and are good swimmers. Sometimes they walk under water along the riverbed and feed.
- Anacondas can weigh more than 100 kilograms. They are the world's heaviest snakes.
- Capybaras are the world's largest rodents. They are about the size of a bulldog. Capybaras are excellent swimmers and can even sleep in the water.

bromeliad

Comprehension questions

1. Describe how the passing of time is shown throughout this book.

2. Name three diurnal predators in the Amazon rainforest, and their prey. Then name three nocturnal predators and their prey.

Glossary

amphibian animal that lives in the water when it is young and can live on land as an adult; frogs and salamanders are amphibians

bromeliad type of tropical plant usually with stiff leaves; some bromeliads get food and water from the air and rain instead of through roots

burrow tunnel or hole in the ground made or used by an animal for shelter

canopy cover formed by the highest layer of branches and leaves in a forest

climate average weather of a place throughout the year

diurnal active during the day

equator imaginary line around the middle of Earth

habitat natural home or environment of an animal, plant or other living thing

mammal any animal of which the female gives birth to live young and can feed them with her own milk

nocturnal active at night

predator animal that hunts other animals

prey animal hunted by another animal

reptile animal whose body temperature changes with its surroundings; most reptiles lay eggs and have scaly skin; snakes, turtles and alligators are reptiles

rodent mammal with long front teeth used for gnawing; rats, mice and squirrels are rodents

talon long, sharp claw of a bird

troop group

Read more

Anaconda (A Day in the Life: Rainforest Animals), Anita Ganeri (Raintree, 2011)

Exploring Rainforests (Exploring Habitats), Anita Ganeri (Raintree, 2014)

Rainforest Food Chains (Food Chains and Webs), Angela Royston (Raintree, 2014)

Living and Non-Living in the Rainforest (Is It Living or Non-living?), Rebecca Rissman (Raintree, 2014)

Index

Websites

www.rainforest-alliance.org/kids/species-profiles/jaguar
Learn all about the Jaguar and other amazing rainforest animals on this fact-filled website.

www.kidsdiscover.com/spotlight/the-amazon-for-kids/
View some stunning photographs of rainforest wildlife on this interesting website, which also gives a great overview of the Amazon rainforest.

Special thanks to our advisers for their expertise, research and advice:

Janalee P. Caldwell, Curator Emeritus & Professor Emeritus, Biology
Sam Noble Museum, University of Oklahoma

Terry Flaherty, PhD, Professor of English
Minnesota State University, Mankato

Raintree is an imprint of Capstone Global Library Limited, a company incorporated in England and Wales having its registered office at 7 Pilgrim Street, London, EC4V 6LB – Registered company number: 6695582

www.raintree.co.uk
myorders@raintree.co.uk

Editorial credits:
Jill Kalz, editor; Lori Bye, designer; Nathan Gassman, art director; Kathy McColley, production specialist

ISBN 978 1 4062 9420 0
18 17 16 15 14
10 9 8 7 6 5 4 3 2 1

British Library Cataloguing in Publication Data
A full catalogue record for this book is available from the British Library.

The illustrations in this book were created with cut paper.
Design Elements: Shutterstock/Alfondo de Tomas (map), Alvaro Cabrera Jimenez

Look out for all the books in the series:

A Day and Night in the Amazon Rainforest

A Day and Night in the Sonoran Desert

Printed in China. 3656